Little Elizabeth

WRITTEN BY
VALERIE WILDING

ILLUSTRATED BY
PAULINE REEVES

wren
& rook

Baby Princess 1926

You may think you know QUEEN ELIZABETH II. She's the lady with the curly, white hair who lives in a palace with her corgis, royal family and beautiful crowns, right?

But once, a very long time ago, the Queen wasn't actually the Queen. She was a young princess who loved to play and have fun.

This is that YOUNG PRINCESS'S STORY.

'Elizabeth'? That's a bit of a mouthful for a little one.

Nursemaid Margaret MacDonald. Nicknamed BOBO.

Clara Knight. Elizabeth couldn't pronounce her first name and called her ALLA.

Over one hundred years ago, two princes were born – Edward and Albert. Their parents were King George V of the United Kingdom and Queen Mary. Edward would become King after his father.

Albert became the Duke of York. He fell in love with a noble lady, called Elizabeth Bowes-Lyon. Albert proposed THREE TIMES before she said, 'Yes'!

On 21 April 1926, Albert and Elizabeth had a baby. She became Her Royal Highness the Princess Elizabeth of York.

She'll probably call herself Lizzie. Or Betty.

Everyone will call her Your Highness or Ma'am, but we'll call her our Lilibet!

PRINCESS ELIZABETH was always meant to stay a princess and never be the Queen. That's because everyone was sure her uncle Edward would become King and that he would marry and have children.

But things don't always work out as you might expect …

Bobo's sister, RUBY.

Growing Up Royal 1930-35

Elizabeth's home was in PICCADILLY, LONDON. It had five floors (that's a lot of stairs!) and a balcony. It was a bit like a SMALL PALACE, except that people going past on buses could see into the windows. Behind the house were gardens that were shared by the neighbours. They must have loved sharing with a princess!

Being a princess meant that Elizabeth had to do princess things such as CURTSYING to her grandparents (can you imagine!).

When her grandfather, King George V, was ill, she used to visit him to cheer him up. For her fourth birthday, he gave Elizabeth her very own pony called PEGGY!

I'll have that lot when she's gone to bed.

Elizabeth adored horses. She had a collection of toy horses on wheels. She lined them all up on the landing and, before bedtime, she would feed and water them.

But soon Elizabeth didn't just have toy horses to play with, she had a little sister called MARGARET ROSE!

The princess had to study lots of subjects including maths and French – though she didn't like them much. Once, when she was fed up with her French lesson, she put a pot of ink upside down on her own head!

Carrots for Blaze, apple for Dolly, cabbage for Bonnie and a mint for Star.

It is ROYAL blue ink, Mamselle.

When I'm a grown-up princess, I shall get someone else to do my sums.

Christmas

The little princesses, Elizabeth and her sister Margaret, had lots of fun playing together at their country home in Windsor, but the best time of the year was CHRISTMAS! Elizabeth spent some of her pocket money buying PRESENTS from Woolworths – a shop that sold everything from sweets and necklaces to pencils and woolly hats.

Granny, your CROWN'S fallen in the gravy.

The Christmas tree was so huge that the staff had to use ladders to decorate it!

Christmas was spent with the King and Queen at Sandringham House in Norfolk. But FATHER CHRISTMAS knew where to find the princesses! They woke on Christmas morning and pounced on their STOCKINGS to see what presents he'd brought them.

After church they had a huge lunch and played an acting game called charades. But everything stopped when it was time for the King to make a SPEECH to his people on the WIRELESS.

By then it was time for TEA, and on with the FUN!

Don't worry, dear. I have another in my JEWEL cupboard.

The Year That Changed Everything 1936

As a YOUNG PRINCESS, Elizabeth expected to GROW UP and live in the countryside, where she could breed her beloved horses. But when she was ten years old, EVERYTHING would change.

Elizabeth's much-loved grandfather, King George V had died soon after Christmas. The new king was Elizabeth's uncle, Edward (though confusingly the family called him David!). He became known as KING EDWARD VIII.

Things did NOT go smoothly ...

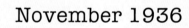

November 1936

Uncle David's girlfriend is an American lady called Wallis Simpson. She's getting divorced so she can be with David. But that's the problem. The King is head of the Church, and the Church people don't let divorced people marry again — especially to the King!

Our maid said the government and the people don't want him to marry Wallis either. But Mummy says he's totally mad about her!

December 1936

Uncle David (King Edward VIII), has made a speech telling the people he's got to stop being King because he loves Wallis too much to give her up. Isn't that romantic!

But hang on ... this means Papa is going to be King! And Mummy will be Queen. And ...

Oh dear oh dear oh dear!
One day ...
I'll be ...
QUEEN!

January 1937

It's strange being the King's daughters. We have to curtsy to Papa! (Though we don't bother when nobody's around.) He's even changed his name. He doesn't want to be King Albert. He wants to be King George, like his own papa. And we have to move to huge draughty old Buckingham Palace. At least our toy horses will have more room — they can have a whole corridor to themselves!

The Coronation 1937

The BIG EVENT of 1937 was the Coronation of Elizabeth's parents at Westminster Abbey. Elizabeth sat next to Queen Mary for the ceremony. It was VERY LONG, and Elizabeth sometimes had to nudge Margaret when she was fidgeting! When she turned a page of her programme and found they were near the end, she and Queen Mary shared a secret smile.

Everyone wore a crown for the coronation. The princesses' golden coronets were specially made for the BIG DAY.

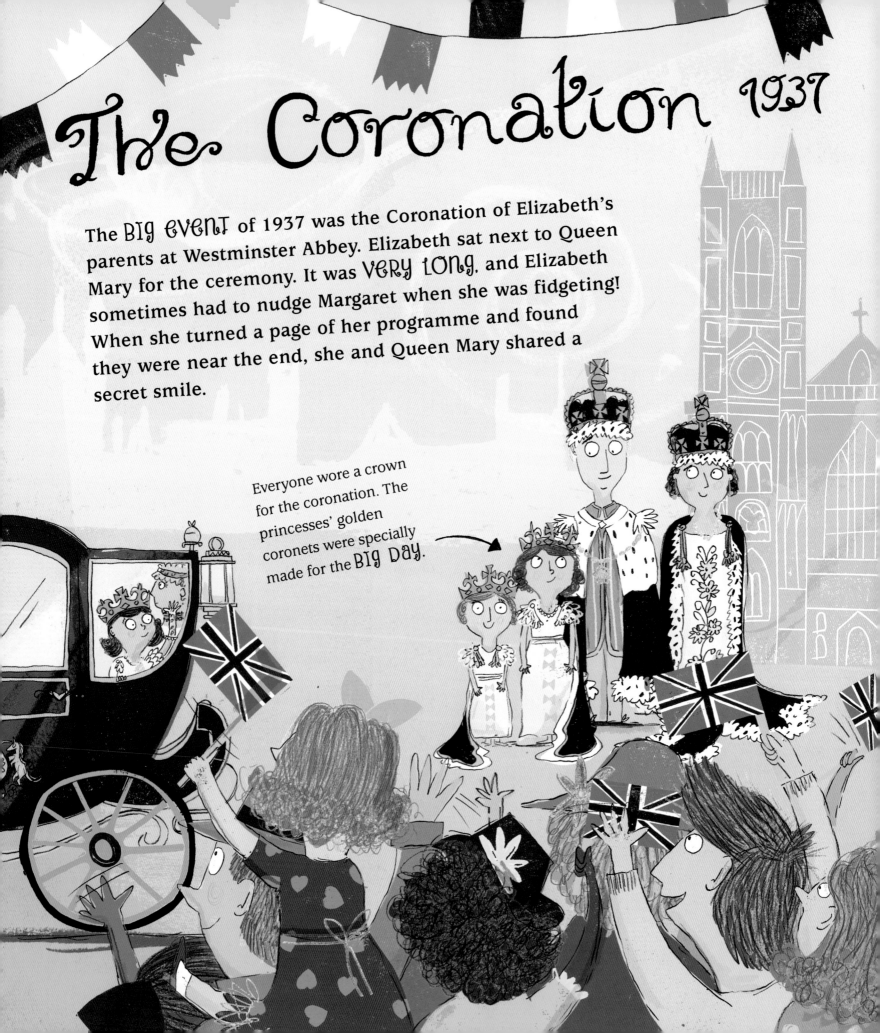

Back at the palace, they waited AGES for the King and Queen to arrive. The royal family went out onto the palace balcony, and Elizabeth could hardly believe her eyes. THOUSANDS of people looked up at them, cheering for her Papa. Then there were photographs to be taken while everybody's tummies rumbled. FINALLY, at nearly six o'clock, TEA!

As a SPECIAL SOUVENIR, Elizabeth made her parents a gift for the occasion. It was her own STORY of the great day.

The Coronation.
12th May, 1937

To Mummy and Papa
In Memory of Their Coronation
From Lilibet

By Herself

I might be King George the Sixth, but I'm your PAPA first.

My arm aches.

Next time, bring a glove on a stick.

What a LOVELY day. My legs are tired, and I'm so slee ... zzzzzzzzz.

Elizabeth's Photo Album

We started Guides at Buckingham Palace. Now I have lots of new friends.

GIRL GUIDE

This is our Guides HQ in the back garden. Margaret's a Brownie.

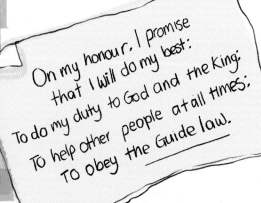

Me at swimming club, rescuing a drowning girl. (Not really drowning, ha ha.)

On my honour, I promise that I will do my best:
To do my duty to God and the king;
To help other people at all times;
To obey the Guide law.

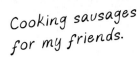

Cooking sausages for my friends.

The seaside's such fun – I wish we could go every day.

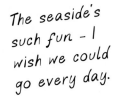

THE ROYAL LIFE SAVING SOCIETY

AWARDED TO ELIZABETH

DOOKIE

My first and cutest pony, Peggy, with the fluffiest mane ever!

Our corgi's real name is Rozavel Golden Eagle, but everyone calls him Dookie because we got him when Papa was Duke of York. They didn't dare call Papa Dookie!

Our budgies. Some of them are friendly. Some of them are pecky.

Our Tibetan Lion Dog. His name is Choo-choo because when he runs he sounds like a steam train! Choo-choo-choo!

Snowball. He doesn't care whether I'm a princess or not. He loves me whatever.

One of my very first horses!

Our weirdest pet, a chameleon (it was a present). Now you see him ...

... now you don't.

Making New Friends 1939

Elizabeth kept busy with school, Guides and swimming. There were lots of outings too, such as RIVERBOAT trips, picnics and a visit to the ROYAL MINT to watch money being made.

Then in July 1939, the family sailed to Devon on the ROYAL YACHT. They visited a college where officers trained for the navy. It didn't look like much fun for a young princess but, for Elizabeth, it turned out VERY HAPPILY ...

OH, LOOK there's Papa's face ... and there ... and there ... and there ...

The Royal Mint

Some of the students have MUMPS, Your Majesty, so this young man will entertain the princesses. Can't let them catch it!

Hmm ... A bit showy-offy. But I like him.

The girls were introduced to **PRINCE PHILIP** of Greece and Denmark. Elizabeth had met him at a wedding when she was eight, but she couldn't remember it!

The three of them played **CROQUET**, and Philip showed off his ability to jump over tennis nets.

She **DEFINITELY** does!

Go back, you nincompoop!

When the royal yacht **SET SAIL**, Philip and other boys followed in small boats, waving goodbye. Soon, everyone except Philip had turned back to shore.

Philip and Elizabeth began writing to each other. But sadly, the **SECOND WORLD WAR** was brewing, which meant Philip would soon be going to sea.

WAR! 1939-40

When war was **DECLARED**, the royal family were in Scotland for the summer. The King and Queen quickly hurried back to London. But the princesses stayed behind at Birkhall, a beautiful house near Balmoral Castle.

Would Yer 'ighness care for a piggyback?

It's an AWFULLY long way down.

Then as the war hotted up, and Britain was badly bombed. Elizabeth and Margaret moved to Windsor Castle, which was strong, with great thick walls. When there was an air raid, they had to **SCURRY** down into a dungeon until it was over!

Elizabeth's Big Speech 1940

The **GOVERNMENT** wanted the Queen to take Elizabeth and Margaret to Canada, where they'd be safe from bombing. But their mother wasn't having that!

The princesses stayed at Windsor instead. But **THOUSANDS** of children were evacuated away from their homes and families. Elizabeth was now fourteen and in October 1940, she made her first speech, on BBC Radio's *Children's Hour* programme.

EXCITING, but scary! Margaret sat silently (for once) as Elizabeth spoke to all the children who'd been evacuated. Elizabeth did her best to sound cheerful and finished by asking Margaret to say '**GOOD NIGHT**', then she added, 'Good night, and good luck to you all.'

How did I do?!

We know what it means to be away from those we love. In the end all will be well.

Panto! 1941-43

CHRISTMAS at Windsor meant PANTOMIME time! Elizabeth and Margaret were the stars. In one of the first pantos, Margaret played Cinderella and Elizabeth was Prince Charming. (Oh yes, she was!)

Local children joined in, and anyone in the castle who could help was roped in to make costumes, music and scenery. The show raised lots of money for the troops.

In 1943, the panto was *Aladdin*. And there was a special guest at Windsor that year ...

Philip was a First Lieutenant in the navy, and he'd grown a beard. He and Elizabeth wrote letters to each other and swapped photos, too.

That's Prince Philip.

Oh NO, it isn't!

Oh YES, it is!

WAR WORK

Elizabeth wanted to do SOMETHING to help in the war. She couldn't work in a factory or nurse sick people, but there was one thing anyone could do. The men fighting the war needed warm clothes, such as scarves, vests and balaclavas. So Elizabeth KNITTED, even though she found it difficult.

Knit one, purl one, drop one, start again ...

When she was SIXTEEN, Elizabeth was old enough to register for war work at the Labour Exchange. Elizabeth desperately wanted to do more for the WAR EFFORT than just knit badly, so she nagged the King to let her get a real job. But the King was worried about her safety. After all, she was expected to be Queen one day.

Suppose the enemy captured you, or a bomb fell on you. WE MUST KEEP YOU SAFE!

All Grown Up 1944-45

On Elizabeth's eighteenth BIRTHDAY in 1944, she was given her own CORGI, which she called Susan. The King had also given her two pearls every year since she was born, and now she had a whole necklace-full!

I wonder what these can be! I do love surprises ...

There were some very IMPORTANT changes now she was eighteen. She was given the grand title Counsellor of State, and if the King was away, she could sign important things, such as new laws. More IMPORTANTLY, if anything bad happened to the King, Elizabeth was now old enough to rule by herself!

She was given staff to work for her, including her very own lady-in-waiting, who would answer letters and go with her when she had to do things – such as open a hospital or launch a SHIP!

SOLDIER PRINCESS

In **1945**, one of Elizabeth's dearest **WISHES** was granted. She'd been nagging the King to let her join the women's branch of the army, the ATS. At last, he said yes! Elizabeth trained as a motor **MECHANIC**. She learned to change wheels and to take engines apart and put them back together again.

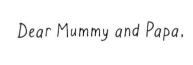

Dear Mummy and Papa,

I love being in the ATS. I really feel I'm doing my bit to help win the war. And it's great being one of the girls.

Well, almost. There's always someone keeping an eye on me, which gets on my nerves. And I wish I was allowed to sleep here like the other girls do. But I must put up with it – I'm heir to the throne, after all.

I'll visit you in Buckingham Palace one day wearing my uniform. Watch out – I might drive myself there! I'm qualified to drive ambulances and trucks now. Not many princesses can do that!

Lots of love from,
230873 second Subaltern Elizabeth Alexandra Mary Windsor

(Lilibet, to you.)

VE Day 1945

The war in Europe came to an end, and in May, Germany surrendered. Londoners went WILD! Boats on the Thames hooted and sirens sounded. Crowds flocked to the Mall in front of Buckingham Palace. They sang, danced, cheered and cried with JOY. 'We want the King!' they shouted, and the royal family went onto the balcony to wave.

Dear Philip,

I know you're somewhere at sea near Japan, so I've no idea when you'll get this. But here it is – VE Day! Victory in Europe! Tonight, thousands of people were celebrating outside the palace and – you'll never believe it – Papa let me and Margaret go out to join them!

Don't worry, some Guards officers looked after us. We wandered miles through the city, and we sang 'Roll Out the Barrel', and danced and cheered! Such fun.

Oh, if only I could have shared the day with you ...

I do miss you. I hope Japan does what Germany did and surrenders soon so you can come home to your loving Lilibet

xxx

Princess in Love 1946

Elizabeth ENJOYED life after the war. She was busy with royal duties but had plenty of fun as well. There were parties and dances. She learned lots about horse racing and breeding. And she LOVED going to race meetings.

In the summer of 1946, Philip was invited to Balmoral and, at last, he proposed! Elizabeth was thrilled and said 'Yes!', but the King and Queen felt she was a little too young. They weren't even sure that Philip was right for her. So the King said that the engagement must be kept SECRET until she was twenty-one.

I'm NOT too young! I want to marry Philip, and I'm jolly well going to! I know Philip's the right man for me!

A SOLEMN PROMISE 1947

Elizabeth's diary

I spent my twenty-first birthday here in Cape Town, South Africa. For a long time now, I've been thinking about how I'll be Queen one day.

Today, I made a speech on the wireless. I spoke to all the people of the British Commonwealth and Empire, and I was pretty nervous because I think it was the most important speech I will ever make. It was my solemn promise to devote my whole life to our people, wherever they are in the world.

I told the people I can't do this alone, and I asked them to join in it with me.

But when I think about it, I won't really be alone. Philip will be beside me.

Royal Wedding

In July 1947, the ENGAGEMENT was announced. Philip's mum gave him some diamonds to make Elizabeth's RING. At last she could let the whole world see it!

Wedding preparations began, and an early GIFT came from the Girl Guides of Australia. They knew that foods such as sugar were rationed because of the war, so they sent ingredients for the wedding cake!

Clothes were rationed, too, so Elizabeth saved her clothing coupons for her WEDDING DRESS. Kind people sent coupons to her too, but they were returned with a thank-you letter. It was against the law to use someone else's coupons.

Today, I shall promise to love, honour and obey my new husband. I'm not too sure about that last bit, though! We'll see.

Right-O Magazine's Royal Wedding Issue!

The dull, CHILLY MORNING of 20 November 1947 was brightened by the red, white and blue of guardsmen's uniforms. MARCHING BANDS and the CHEERS of the waiting crowds almost drowned out the sound of clattering hooves and jangling harnesses.

Philip leaves Kensington Palace with the good wishes of a LUCKY chimney sweep ringing in his ears!

And here she is! Doesn't she look HAPPY!

We talked to people waiting outside Westminster Abbey. 'They say the dress has 10,000 pearls sewn on it,' one woman said.

The princess is stunning in ivory silk, embroidered with flowers. The train is four metres long and the star-embroidered veil is topped by a diamond tiara. The proud father looks on!

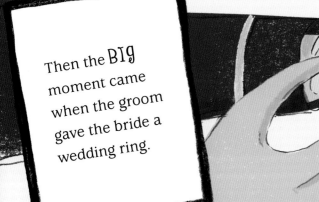

Then the **BIG** moment came when the groom gave the bride a wedding ring.

That ring was made using Welsh gold from a nugget given to the bride's mother for her own wedding.

BELLS CHIMED as the couple left the abbey and headed home in the Glass Coach. Thousands of voices cheered them on their way. And then it was time for the wedding breakfast.

Menu

Filet de Sole Mountbatten

Perdreau en Casserole

Bombe Glacée

Princess Elizabeth pudding

E P

Most princesses have a ship or a rose named after them. Elizabeth's namesake is a **PUDDING!**

The newlyweds leave for their **HONEYMOON** which begins in the Hampshire countryside and continues in Birkhall, in Scotland.

A honeymoon for two?

WOOF!

Wow! Over 2,500 wedding **PRESENTS** – mini dolls of Elizabeth and Philip, jewels, an ostrich egg, paintings, handbags, sewing machines, and more!

November 1947

A New Life 1947-52

The country home the NEWLYWEDS planned to live in burnt down before the wedding – disaster! But they still had their London home, Clarence House, and there was more big news to come …

On 14 November 1948, Prince Charles was born. A future king!

CONGRATULATIONS ON YOUR NEW HOME

Oh heck, look at the state of that!

A NEW HOME

Never mind, we'll stay with Mummy and Papa until it's fixed.

The King became ill, and everyone was worried. But Elizabeth had some good news for him.

Get Well Soon

I'm going to have a baby, Papa!

You can tell he's royal. He's learned to wave already.

Philip was posted to a ship in the Mediterranean, so Elizabeth was left at home with the baby.

farewell!

Elizabeth went to visit Philip on the island of Malta. Little Charles stayed with his grandparents.

In 1950 there was lots to celebrate. The couple had another baby, Princess Anne, and Philip was made captain of his own ship.

I'm not staying here by myself. I'll go and visit Philip as soon as I can.

I'm having a wonderful time. I do miss baby Charles, though.

Coronation 1953

A queen needs a *CROWN*, and on 2 June 1953, Elizabeth woke to a *RAINY CORONATION DAY*. Excited spectators camped overnight ready to cheer her procession. Elizabeth rode in the Gold State Coach to be crowned in Westminster Abbey and, for the first time ever, millions of people watched it all happen on live TV!

The **QUEEN'S** arrived!

Is it *NEARLY* finished?

Over **8,000** guests attended the coronation at Westminster Abbey – even Prince Charles, who was four years old at the time.

THE QUEEN'S GOWN was embroidered with the English Tudor rose, Scottish thistle, Welsh leek and Northern Irish shamrock. The designer slipped in one extra four-leafed clover for luck. Elizabeth didn't know!

THE ST. EDWARD'S CROWN is the coronation crown. It's made of solid gold and is decorated with 444 sparkling jewels.

Later, Elizabeth wore the **IMPERIAL STATE CROWN.** It contains over 3,000 jewels and Elizabeth once said that if she leaned forward, it would break her neck!

THE ORB is a globe that represents the world, with a cross that symbolises the Christian faith.

THE CORONATION RING is known as 'the wedding ring of England'.

The Queen sat in **ST EDWARD'S CHAIR** to be crowned. It's been used in every coronation for 700 years.

THE SCEPTRE, a symbol of power and justice, holds the world's largest cut diamond!

The young princess who grew up to be Queen could never have imagined that she would rule her people for **LONGER** than any other king or queen in the whole of British history. But that's just what she's done.

So, she's not only a fantastic queen, she's also a

RECORD-BREAKER!

GLOSSARY

air raid bombing attacks on Britain by the German air force

british commonwealth a family of nations that has the Queen as its head

balaclavas a warm, woolly covering for the head and neck, with holes for eyes, mouth or whole face

ceremony an important occasion, performed in a special way

coronation a ceremony when a king or queen is crowned

empire a group of countries ruled by one person or government

evacuated when children were sent to live somewhere safe during wartime

rationed when food or clothing is shared equally

surrendered when the losing side in a war has given up the fight

wireless the old name for a radio

For Marilyn Malin, with love and thanks. – V.W.
For my Mum, Beate, for always treating me like her little princess. – P.R.

First published in Great Britain in 2021
by Wren & Rook

Text copyright © Valerie Wilding, 2021
Illustration copyright © Pauline Reeves, 2021

The right of Valerie Wilding and Pauline Reeves to
be identified as author and illustrator respectively
of this work has been asserted by them in accordance
with the Copyright, Designs and Patents Act 1988.

Hardback ISBN: 978 1 5263 6299 5
Paperback ISBN: 978 1 5263 6300 8
E-book ISBN: 978 1 5263 6301 5
10 9 8 7 6 5 4 3 2 1

FSC MIX Paper from responsible sources FSC® C104740
www.fsc.org

Wren & Rook
An imprint of
Hachette Children's Group
Part of Hodder & Stoughton
Carmelite House
50 Victoria Embankment
London EC4Y 0DZ
An Hachette UK Company
www.hachette.co.uk
www.hachettechildrens.co.uk

Publishing Director: Debbie Foy
Commissioning Editor: Laura Horsley
Art Director: Laura Hambleton
Senior Designer: Sophie Gordon

Printed in China